For my Mom and Dad...

Special thanks to Richie Swann, Michael Beford, Judson Lindsay, Jean Anne Jordan, Brett McKee, Josh Campbell, Katie Miller, Randy Bates Jr. & Sr., Adam Ferell, Ducan-Parnell, Wonder Works, Piggly Wiggly, The Charleston RiverDogs, SC Aquarium, Barry K., Charleston Green Home, the marketing departments of College of Charleston and The Citadel, Angela Mallen, and the good people at Artist & Craftsman Supply, who keep me knee deep in construction paper!

Published by Underdog Endeavor Productions, LLC. Charleston, SC
Printed by Pacom in South Korea

ISBN - 10: 0981952321
ISBN - 13: 978-0-9819523-2-1

For more information please go to:
sammydogbooks.com

The ADVENTURES of SAMMY

the Wonder Dachshund

Best Wishes! Sammy

Sammy's Last Week in Charleston

Story and Illustrations by Jonathan D. Miller

Sunday

Early Sunday morning, Sammy got out of bed, stretched his paws, and yawned a big yawn. He went to the kitchen to make his favorite food, scrambled eggs. Sammy quickly cooked a hefty plate of eggs because he couldn't wait to get out to the beach to play with all of his friends. But as he sat down to eat, his big, floppy ears perked up. The phone rang...

Sammy's boss was calling to tell Sammy that his new job would require him to move far away from Charleston. Sammy knew it was a good opportunity, so he agreed to move. But as he began to eat, he became very sad. He thought about how much he loved Charleston and all his wonderful friends. Sammy began to worry.

Sammy realized that he had lived in Charleston for quite some time, but he still hadn't done a lot of things he wanted to. Sammy knew he had only one week left. He didn't want to miss out on anything, so he sat down and wrote out a list of things to do before he moved.

Sammy knew he would have to hurry to fit it all in to one week. He finished his breakfast and went to the beach on Sullivan's Island to tell his friends about his exciting news.

Monday

Sammy left his house and walked to the Battery. He sat on a park bench and looked out over the water toward Fort Sumter. It was such a pretty day, and the view was incredible. He thought about how much he loved coming here to relax, run, or play catch.

Sammy wanted to buy some gifts from stores on King Street for his friends. Along the way, he stopped to take a picture of the houses on Rainbow Row for his mom because he really liked their colors.

Sammy spent the rest of the afternoon shopping on King Street. He bought so many presents for his family and friends that he needed a big wagon to get them all home.

Tuesday

Sammy woke up and realized he had no eggs for breakfast, so he went to the grocery store to buy some. While he was there, he also bought supplies to help with his move.

The next thing on Sammy's list was a visit to the South Carolina Aquarium, where he learned a lot about the ocean and marine life. He touched a starfish and saw sharks and eels. He had so much fun he spent the whole day there.

wednesday

Sammy stopped at The Citadel Military College to say goodbye to some friends. He marched around the school and took pictures of the beautiful campus.

Sammy had such a great time at The Citadel, he decided to visit his friends at the College of Charleston as well. As he sat on the Cistern, he wagged his tail and thought about the fun he had learning so much in college.

That night Sammy had a nice, quiet, going-away dinner with some of his closest friends at his favorite restaurant. He ate so much wonderful food that he had to be rolled home.

Thursday

Sammy went out to Folly Beach one last time. He surfed and played in the water. He collected seashells and sharks teeth to take to his new home. When Sammy left the beach, he saw that his friends had painted a message for him on the abandoned boat.

On the way home, Sammy stopped by Wonder Works to pick up a few of his favorite toys and to give the Wonder Workers each one last hug.

Later that afternoon, he met some friends for a baseball game. Sammy loves

baseball, and the Charleston RiverDogs are his favorite team.

Friday

The next adventure on Sammy's list was to visit the Angel Oak. He had only seen pictures of the big tree in books but had never seen it in person. He drove out to the Angel Oak and stood admiring the size of the tree and its beauty.

That evening, Sammy jogged to Colonial Lake. He sat by the water and
watched the sunset.

Saturday

Sammy went to meet friends at Marion Square. After playing, Sammy wanted to get a good view of the city, so he climbed the statue in the middle of the park.

From the top of the statue, he could see all of downtown Charleston. For the first time, he saw all the church steeples at once and understood why people call Charleston the Holy City.

Sammy looked at his list and realized he only had one thing left to do.

Sammy had been so busy that he hadn't had a chance to say goodbye to his best friend. Sammy called her and together they strolled to the Cooper River Bridge. They walked to the middle of the bridge. There, they looked out over the water and talked for hours. The sun was beginning to set, so Sammy walked her to her door. He smiled, told her how much he would miss her, and said, "Goodbye."

Sunday

Sunday morning, the movers came and loaded everything that Sammy owned into the moving truck. When Sammy walked outside, all of his friends were waiting to give him gifts and hugs and to say their goodbyes.

As Sammy drove away, he began to cry. It was hard for him to leave his friends and such a wonderful city.

But while he thought about all the things that he did over the past week, he began to smile.

Sammy knew that he would always have great friends in Charleston and that he could visit anytime.

Sammy was no longer sad at all...

Because he realized he was not saying goodbye to Charleston forever. He was just saying, "See you soon."

Illustrator's Note:

All the illustrations in The Adventures of Sammy the Wonder Dachshund series are made by layering cut-out pieces of colored construction paper and card stock. These shapes are arranged to form a much bigger picture and then are given a little detail with the use of a Sharpie marker. It takes an average of 30 to 40 hours to construct each page.

Here is a simplified example of the process:

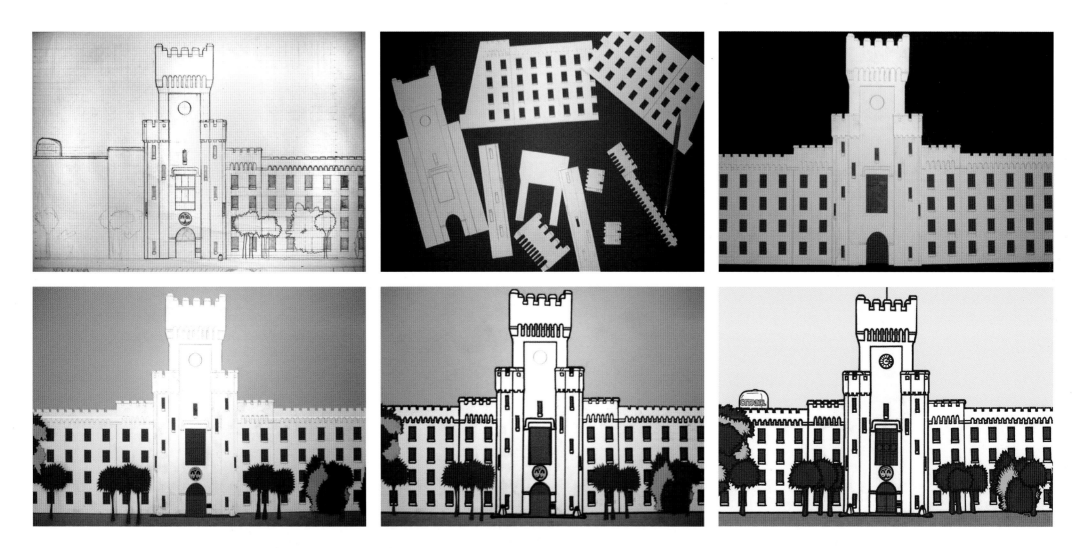

I hope you enjoy the pictures as much as I loved making them. -Jonathan D. Miller

See more artwork at sammydogbooks.com.

If you want to read about Sammy's next adventure, get a copy of Sammy on Safari today!

sammydogbooks.com